W9-BMK-039

MENTORING:
A PRACTICAL GUIDE
Revised Edition

Gordon F. Shea

A FIFTY-MINUTE™ SERIES BOOK

CRISP PUBLICATIONS, INC.
Menlo Park, California

MAR 12 1998

MENTORING:
A PRACTICAL GUIDE
Revised Edition

Gordon F. Shea

CREDITS
Managing Editor: **Kathleen Barcos**
Editor: **Tony Hicks**
Production: **Leslie Power**
Typesetting: **ExecuStaff**
Cover Design: **Carol Harris**

All rights reserved. No part of this book may be reproduced or transmitted in any form or by any means now known or to be invented, electronic or mechanical, including photocopying, recording, or by any information storage or retrieval system without written permission from the author or publisher, except for the brief inclusion of quotations in a review.

Copyright © 1992, 1997 by Crisp Publications.

Printed in the United States of America by Bawden Printing Company.

Distribution to the U.S. Trade:

National Book Network, Inc.
4720 Boston Way
Lanham, MD 20706
1-800-462-6420

Library of Congress Catalog Card Number 97-66608
Shea, Gordon F.
Mentoring
ISBN 1-56052-426-X

10 9 8 7 6 5 4 3 2 1

This book is printed on recyclable paper with soy ink.

LEARNING OBJECTIVES FOR:

MENTORING: REVISED EDITION

The objectives for *Mentoring—Revised Edition* are listed below. They have been developed to guide you, the reader, to the core issues covered in this book.

Objectives

❑ 1) **To explain how anyone can assist the growth of other people**

❑ 2) **To suggest mentor behaviors to adopt or avoid**

❑ 3) **To show how mentoring works in today's workplace**

Assessing Your Progress

In addition to the Learning Objectives, *Mentoring—Revised Edition* includes a unique new **assessment tool*** which can be found at the back of this book. A twenty-five item, multiple choice/true-false questionnaire allows the reader to evaluate his or her comprehension of the subject matter covered. An answer sheet, with a chart matching the questions to the listed objectives, is also provided.

* Assessments should not be used in any selection process.

INTRODUCTION

This book lays a solid foundation for developing successful mentor behaviors. It enables the reader to identify and assess his or her own mentoring experiences—as mentor or mentee—and to use mentoring as an empowering tool for positive employee and personal development. The book also deals with the practical aspects of mentoring, i.e., what makes mentoring special, assessing what the mentor is able and willing to invest in the relationship and the special opportunities and challenges of mentoring in various special situations today and tomorrow—cross cultural, cross-gender, and supervisor/employee mentoring.

The how-to-do-it sections of the book deal with understanding mentee needs, positive mentor behaviors, behaviors to avoid, and ways to make the most of the mentor/mentee relationship in the short and long run.

This publication can be used as an individual workbook for exploring mentoring, or as a series of pre- or post-exercises to supplement a course on mentoring. Many of the exercises provide a basis for classroom or small group discussion.

Gordon F. Shea

Gordon F. Shea

CONTENTS

men•tor / 'men-,to(ə)r, 'ment-ər / *n* [L, fr. Gk *Mentor*] **1** *cap* : a friend of Odysseus entrusted with the education of Telemachus **2** : a trusted counselor or guide **3** : TUTOR, COACH.

THERE IS A NEW FORM OF MENTORING EVOLVING THAT BETTER SUITS THE DOWN-SIZED, HIGH-TECH, GLOBALLY COMPETITIVE FIRMS THAT ARE EMERGING IN OUR SOCIETY.

THE CONCEPT OF MENTORING IS NO LONGER TAILORED TO THE TALL, HEIRARCHICAL ORGANIZATIONS. THAT OLD MILIEU WAS PATERNALISTIC AND NURTURED THE STATUS QUO.

MENTORING IS NOW SEEN AS A PROCESS WHEREBY MENTOR AND MENTEE WORK TOGETHER TO DISCOVER AND DEVELOP THE MENTEE'S LATENT ABILITIES.

THE GOAL IS NOT A PARTICULAR POSITION IN THE COMPANY. RATHER IT IS EMPOWERMENT OF THE MENTEE BY DEVELOPING HIS OR HER ABILITIES.

C H A P T E R

1

Mentoring As An Art

THE STORY OF MENTOR

The story of Mentor comes from Homer's *Odyssey*. When Odysseus, king of Ithaca, went to fight in the Trojan War, he entrusted the care of his household to Mentor, who served as teacher and overseer of Odysseus' son, Telemachus.

After the war, Odysseus was condemned to wander vainly for ten years in his attempt to return home. In time, Telemachus, now grown, went in search of his father. Telemachus was accompanied on his quest by Athena, Goddess of War and patroness of the arts and industry, who assumed the form of Mentor.

Eventually, father and son were reunited and together they cast down would-be usurpers of Odysseus' throne and of Telemachus's birthright. In time the word *Mentor* became synonymous with trusted advisor, friend, teacher, and wise person. History offers many examples of helpful mentoring relationships—such as Socrates and Plato, Hayden and Beethoven, Freud and Jung.

Mentoring is a fundamental form of human development where one person invests time, energy, and personal know-how in assisting the growth and ability of another person.

History and legend record the deeds of princes and kings, but each of us has a birthright to be all that we can be. Mentors are those special people in our lives who, through their deeds and work, help us to move toward fulfilling that potential.

HAVE YOU BEEN MENTORED?

HAVE YOU BEEN MENTORED?

Consider for a moment the following three questions regarding important changes in your life. In answering them, do not focus on the external events. Concentrate on the developments or changes that occurred *within* you—the way you saw yourself, others or events.

1. Who provided an "aha!" experience that allowed you to pierce the core of meaning of some event, in someone, in something, or in yourself? Write about one such experience in the space below:

_____

_____

_____

_____

_____

2. Who provided you with a quote that had great meaning for you, that influenced your thinking or behavior, and that you sometimes repeat? Write down one such quotable quote and where it came from:

_____

_____

_____

_____

_____

3. Who helped you uncover an aspect, an ability, or a talent of yours that, until then, had lain dormant and unrecognized? Describe one such incident:

_____

_____

_____

_____

_____

HELPING AGENTS

Mentors are helpers. Their styles may range from that of a persistent encourager who helps us build our self-confidence, to that of a stern taskmaster who teaches us to appreciate excellence in performance. Whatever their style, they care about us and what we are trying to do.

We can learn much about mentoring from studying those who have affected our lives and the lives of others. Mentor's job was not merely to raise Telemachus, but to *develop* him for the responsibilities he was to assume in his lifetime. Mentors still pursue similar tasks.

Mentoring is also one of the broadest methods of encouraging human growth. Today we often relate mentoring to our careers, but mentors can touch every facet of our being if we take their offerings and apply them in various aspects of our lives.

We may not divorce our career aspirations from other aspects of our development as human beings, citizens, and members of our employing organization. To gain from mentoring, a person has to reach out, grasp, and draw into himself or herself the lessons that mentors offer. The mentee can only *experience* the beneficial gifts of mentoring by assuming ownership of what the mentor has offered.

FROM LEGEND TO CHALLENGE

Mentors are people who have a *special* or *memorable* helpful effect on us and our lives. In each of the areas listed below, write the name of one person who had such an influence on you. Code the person's name if you wish, or use only the first name. If you cannot think of a person for a given area, go on and come back to that item later if someone occurs to you.

Mentors who make important contributions to our:

- Knowledge of how societal systems, processes or things work

  _____

- Values

  _____

- Technical competence

  _____

- Growth in character

  _____

- Knowledge of how to behave in a social situation

  _____

- Understanding of the world around us

  _____

- Understanding of how to get things done in *or* through our organization

  _____

- Moral development

  _____

- Mental and physical health and fitness

  _____

- Understanding of other people and their viewpoint

  _____

- Just about anything else you can think of

  _____

NEW VISIONS

Traditionally in our society mentoring was thought of as a formal process whereby an older, more experienced person helps and guides a younger person in learning the ropes in an organization or on the job. The term *mentoring* has also been used to describe the activities of a senior person in preparing a junior for a particular office or job, providing career guidance, and encouraging high standards of performance. When successful, mentoring was seen to have an important and beneficial effect on a person's career and life.

Mentors were also seen as senior people in an organization who took talented young people under their wing and protected, taught, and even sponsored these protégés. However, in recent years this sponsoring role has been criticized for leading to favoritism, career climbing, and internal politics. In today's globally competitive organizations, many people dislike the word *protégé* and prefer the more neutral term *mentee*.

The traditional career orientation of mentoring, while recognized as important, is seen today as too limiting.

You may be, or may become, involved in a formal mentoring relationship, as designated by your organization or developed by you as a voluntary activity. There are many opportunities to practice spontaneous or informal mentoring. Such relationships can be short or long. *Reasons to Be a Mentor*

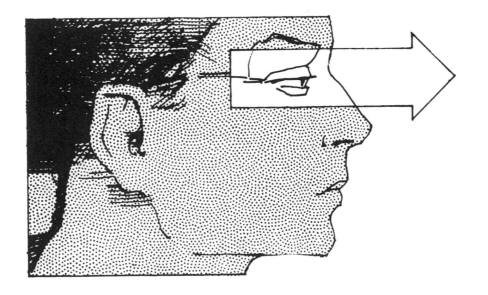

A VARIETY OF MENTORING RELATIONSHIPS

Describe one relationship you have experienced, observed or known about for each of the four categories shown below:

Highly Structured

1. **Highly structured, short-term.** The relationship is formally estabished for an introductory or short period, often to meet specific organization objectives. For example, a new employee may be paired with a senior person for company orientation.

2. **Highly structured, long-term.** Often used for succession planning, this relationship involves grooming someone to take over a departing person's job or function or to master a craft.

3. **Informal, short-term.** This type of off-the-cuff mentoring ranges from one-shot or spontaneous help to occasional or as-needed counseling. There may be no ongoing relationship. This type of intervention is often thought through and heavily change-oriented.

4. **Informal, long-term.** "Friendship mentoring" consists of being available as needed to discuss problems, to listen, or to share special knowledge.

Formality of Relationship

Virtually No Structure

Short-Term Spontaneous

Long-Term Even for Life

Length of Intervention

VARIETY IN BEHAVIORS

Mentoring can be defined as: a significant, long-term, beneficial effect on the life or style of another person, generally as a result of personal one-on-one contact. A mentor is one who offers knowledge, insight, perspective, or wisdom that is especially useful to the other person.

Mentoring can be done by anyone, at any time, and in almost any place. Mentoring can be a one-shot intervention or a lifelong relationship. It can be carried out informally, as part of a friendship, or formally, as part of a highly structured new employee orientation program. Many people who have been mentored recognize that something very special has happened, but they may not have even known what to call the experience.

Often, mentoring is a process whereby mentor and mentee work together to discover and develop the mentee's latent abilities, to provide the mentee with knowledge and skills as opportunities and needs arise, and for the mentor to serve as an effective tutor, counselor, friend and foil who enables the mentee to sharpen skills and hone her or his thinking.

Mentoring can also be almost unconscious. One person may, without realizing it, do or say something which has an important effect on another person. Or the recipient may only become slowly aware of how important a given intervention has been in his or her life. Yet these empowering linkages are not just beneficial accidents. Their power springs from the giving nature of the mentor and the receptiveness of the mentee to absorb, digest and use the lessons passed to her or him.

Probably we have all had such experiences, both as mentor and as mentee.

WHAT MENTORS DO

Following is a list of things that mentors do. As appropriate for each one, check "Others have done this for me" or "I've done this for others" (or both):

Mentors . . .	Others have done this for me	I've done this for others
Set high expectations of performance	❑	❑
Offer challenging ideas	❑	❑
Help build self-confidence	❑	❑
Encourage professional behavior	❑	❑
Offer friendship	❑	❑
Confront negative behaviors and attitudes	❑	❑
Listen to personal problems	❑	❑
Teach by example	❑	❑
Provide growth experiences	❑	❑
Offer quotable quotes	❑	❑
Explain how the organization works	❑	❑
Coach their mentees	❑	❑
Stand by their mentees in critical situations	❑	❑
Offer wise counsel	❑	❑
Encourage winning behavior	❑	❑
Trigger self-awareness	❑	❑
Inspire their mentees	❑	❑
Share critical knowledge	❑	❑
Offer encouragement	❑	❑
Assist with their mentees' careers	❑	❑

A POTENT LIFE EXPERIENCE

In his autobiography, *Confessions of an SOB* (Doubleday, 1989), Al Neuharth, founder of the newspaper *USA Today*, told a poignant story about mentoring.

Neuharth moved to Detroit to become assistant to Lee Hill, executive editor of the *Detroit Free Press*. Shortly after his arrival he was invited to lunch by Jack Knight, owner of the Knight-Rider newspaper chain, of which the *Detroit Free Press* was a part. They went around the corner to the posh Detroit Club where they had a cocktail. Then Jack Knight said, "Let's go."

A surprised Neuharth said, "Aren't we going to have lunch?"

Knight said, "Yeah, let's go."

Al was led six blocks to the basement lunch counter in the old Woolworth Five and Dime store. There, Jack Knight ordered a hot dog and coke and asked Neuharth what he wanted. Al had the same. Here was this immaculately dressed multimillionaire, a Pulitzer Prize–winning writer in his own right, and one of America's most powerful media moguls, handing Al a hot dog with mustard and ketchup.

Knight then said, in effect: Lee Hill will give you memberships in the Detroit Club and the Athletic Club and take you to meet the mayor and a lot of other civic leaders, and after a while you will think you are writing for them. But remember, a lot of people who buy our papers eat here every day. Ask them what they read. "Remember," Knight continued, "don't become a captive of your own comfort. Keep your feet on the street. And don't eat at the Detroit Club every day."

Neuharth relates that experience directly to the thinking that years later went into the design of *USA Today* as a popular national tabloid.

This type of powerful life experience is, in a situational sense, what mentoring is all about. Mentors provide exceptional learning experiences for their mentees and highlight the key ideas and information that make events memorable and meaningful. They expand their mentees' awareness, insight, and perspective. They can be a powerful force for developing employees and their organization. There is often a bit of improvisation and drama in the mentoring experiences which we remember and use.

SHARING LIFE EXPERIENCE

Write your answers in the spaces provided:

1. Who arranged an unusual learning experience for you that allowed you to see into another sphere of life or to look behind the scenes? Describe one such episode.

_____
_____
_____
_____
_____
_____

2. Describe the most unusual mentoring experience you have encountered, and indicate its importance to you.

_____
_____
_____
_____
_____
_____

3. Identify one situation where you could (or did) provide an unusual experience for another person, which would open new vistas for them, enable them to see how other people live, or help them see something important in a new light.

_____
_____
_____
_____
_____
_____

SPECIAL HELPERS

Even formal mentoring is largely the art of *making the most of a given situation.* This flexible view tends to distress some individuals, who expect and perhaps need a cookbook approach to any task. They want to know exactly what they are supposed to do, how to do it and when to do it.

To tell them that mentoring is part intuition, part feelings and part hunch—made up as you go along, and composed of whatever ingredients you have available at the moment—is too uncertain for them. But that is largely what it is, and from that reality it derives its power.

For example, a person who learns counseling skills can become a counselor, and *perhaps* a mentor. But mentoring would occur only when the counselor creates an intervention in the relationship that goes beyond counseling; otherwise the word *mentoring* has no special meaning. Therefore, helping a subordinate cope with his or her mate's alcoholism is not necessarily mentoring—it is more like counseling. But even a casual remark, if it reveals a new facet of a problem, could be mentoring, whether it is made by a counselor or anyone else.

This special spark, which reveals new aspects of things in a flash, is often missing in today's education and training. Fortunately, it is often provided by people other than educators and trainers—people who care enough about the person to make it happen. Mentoring goes beyond what we normally learn in schools.

Why are today's organizational leaders so interested in promoting a type of relationship which is so amorphous and random? Because in an increasingly complex and high-tech environment, we all experience needs for special insight, understanding and information that are outside the normal channels or training programs. There may be someone around us who can help fill in the cracks in our comprehension of the complex problems we face. These special people are our mentors.

LIFE HELPERS

IDENTIFYING OUR LIFE HELPERS

Identify three people who have significantly and beneficially influenced you. Describe what they have contributed to your life:

1. Someone who has inspired you to shift the direction of your life in a constructive way.

_____

_____

_____

_____

2. Someone who has provided something to help you grow in depth of feeling, character, or moral or ethical integrity, or who has helped you develop a deeper commitment to your values.

_____

_____

_____

_____

3. Someone who has provided some form of help to you at *just the right time.*

_____

_____

_____

_____

Were any of these assists a spontaneous response to a great need of yours—whether you had recognized the need at the time or not? If so, which?

_____

_____

_____

_____

THE EXTRA MILE

Except in formal mentoring programs where a mentor may be assigned to guide a mentee, the mentoring relationship is not duty bound. Teachers who dispense information under contract or lawyers who tender wise counsel for a fee are merely doing their jobs. Mentoring is more than doing a job—it is help that goes beyond obligatory relationships.

Teachers can mentor and so can lawyers. The difference between a teacher and a great teacher is often due to the extra mentoring component that some people offer. Most of us have known many good and competent teachers who do their work with art and style. The fortunate ones among us have also encountered teachers who have lit a spark within us, who opened new vistas and dimensions before us, who touched us deeply and who awakened and encouraged our potential.

Similarly, a senior lawyer might take a younger person, fresh from the bar exam, under her wing. She might teach the novice the ropes of the lawyering trade, set high standards of performance, call her mentee to meet the most exacting professional codes, and provide encouragement and comfort during the tough initial period of getting one's feet on the ground in the law firm.

Mentoring involves going above and beyond. It is a relationship in which a person with greater experience, expertise, and wisdom counsels, teaches, guides, and helps another person to develop both personally and professionally.

But what of the senior person in an organization who has been assigned the task of mentoring a junior person in a formal mentoring program? If that person performs his duties in a perfunctory fashion, although holding the *title* of mentor, he will miss the essence of the experience.

REACHING OUT TO ANOTHER PERSON

Mentoring is often the extra increment that makes the difference to a mentee.

Relate one experience where you reached out to another person who was deeply in need, and your help appeared to make a beneficial difference to that person.

_____

_____

_____

_____

_____

Describe one experience you observed, read or heard about where someone reached out to another person to help in an unusual way. It need not be as dramatic as the Neuharth story, but it often has an imaginative or unusual twist to it, which helped make the experience memorable and of continuing utility.

_____

_____

_____

_____

_____

Describe one mentoring experience you have had which did not fit the direct, one-on-one personal aspect of mentoring. For example, a special parental message, a quote from literature, a speech, a sermon, etc.

_____

_____

_____

_____

_____

CHAPTER

2

Is Mentoring For You?

INVESTING IN OTHERS

Are you ready, willing, and able to mentor others? Are you emotionally and psychologically prepared to invest time and effort in helping another person? Are you ready to make such a commitment? Do you have the time, the skills, the freedom to devote yourself to another person?

To mentor is to change your life, if only in small ways. Impromptu, off-the-cuff mentoring requires at least a heightened awareness of the needs of others and a willingness to pause or listen for a while. Taking on a formal mentoring assignment at work may mean occasional inconveniences and less time for other duties. Mentoring a young person as a community effort can conflict with family commitments and activities. Mentoring can also mean substantial personal change—perhaps a willingness to listen more and talk less, or less time for a favorite sport or recreation.

Mentoring that causes you significant stress or loss in other areas should be weighed carefully before you make a commitment. Yet, if you are ready, the personal satisfaction may be well worth the time and effort expended—"eyes open" is the watchword.

Mentors also need to believe in the value of their work without worrying about returned favors. If you have, or can develop, a freely giving nature, you will probably be mentoring for all your life—probably without thinking much about it.

YOUR INVESTMENT IN MENTORING

Mentoring can range from a spur-of-the-moment intervention to an intense long-term relationship. We need to assess where we are at the moment— recognizing that conditions and our interests may need to be reappraised from time to time.

The mentee's needs and mentor's resources vary over time, reflecting the complexities of life.

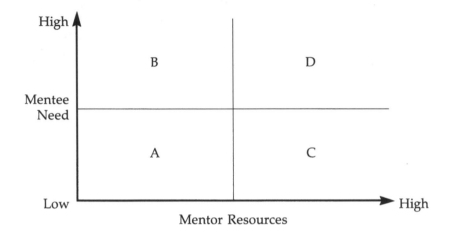

Quadrant A: The mentor's resources and mentee's needs are low, spontaneous, or occasional. Very short-term interventions may be adequate and satisfying to both parties.

Quadrant B: The mentee's need is high and the mentor's resources, time, skills, etc., are low. Helping the mentee find a more appropriate mentor (or professional help) may be appropriate, perhaps through a referral to someone in your network.

Quadrant C: The mentor's resources are substantial, but the mentee's needs are low. Occasional help may be all that is needed, and the mentor may have time and talents available for helping others.

Quadrant D: The mentee's need is high and the mentor's resources are abundant. The potential exists for an intense and productive relationship.

The mentor's and mentee's willingness, readiness, and appropriateness need to be judged according to the individual situation. A very willing mentor trying to work with a mentee who perceives little need for help can be inappropriate. Similarly, a needy mentee and an overloaded mentor may not work well together.

SHARING OUR RESOURCES

Mentors bring a variety of resources to a mentoring event or situation. These may vary according to our job, our personality, our interests, our experiences, our network of friends and associates, and our available time and energy. In the spaces below, identify some of your special assets that you bring to a mentoring situation. List one or more items in each category.

My position or work experience: _____

_____

_____

Things I like to do: _____

_____

_____

My education, training and/or experience: _____

_____

_____

My pastimes, hobbies and/or clubs: _____

_____

_____

My special skills and knowledge: _____

_____

_____

My special passion(s): _____

_____

_____

Any other asset: _____

_____

_____

_____

THE EMPOWERING MENTOR

Sound mentoring respects the uniqueness of the mentee and strives to enhance the special strengths of that person. Effective mentors tend to focus on *what* the mentee does in response to the mentor's help rather than *how* he or she does it. Barring some negative or destructive response that might damage the mentee or others, mentors need to focus on the positive results of a transaction—if they are visible.

The desire to "do it my way" is critical to a mentee's sense of self, for it respects that person's specialness. Doing something the mentor's way may lessen mentee ownership. It may be a way for the mentee to avoid thought or responsibility. It may also be downright uncomfortable for the mentee. The mentee should adapt the mentor's help to her own situation and style. This enables the mentee to wrestle with the details, perhaps try different approaches, and discover her own talents or strengths.

Because a mentee may choose to do something her own way and not appear to do what we expected, we may not recognize that our mentoring has been effective. An effective mentor lets go or, more importantly, does not take charge of the mentee. A helping relationship is a freeing relationship. Mentee effectiveness largely hinges on designing their own best way.

NON-DIRECTIVE WAYS OF MENTORING

Identify three situations where you have served or could serve as an effective role model.

1. _____
2. _____
3. _____

Identify two positive attitudes you display, and two ways you help others to overcome negative feelings about themselves.

Positive attitudes:

1. _____
2. _____

Helping others:

1. _____
2. _____

How comfortable do you feel just listening to people with problems?

_____

Plain listening can help mentees let go of their negative feelings. What two types of listening do you do best?

1. _____
2. _____

People seldom want to be told what they should do or how to do it, but an idea or a bit of information offered in a neutral way becomes something they can identify and use. Assess your own ability to share ideas and information in a neutral context.

_____
_____
_____
_____

MENTOR SELF-DEVELOPMENT

Some of the best mentors are persons who assume that they, as well as their mentees, are in a lifelong process of self-development. Long ago, or so it seems, a person could develop a certain level of wisdom and sophistication and pass on what he had learned to those younger and/or less experienced. But each day our world changes and the pace of change accelerates. Therefore we need to decide what types of mentoring we might practice most successfully and what knowledge and skills we need to develop to stay up-to-date.

Focus on basic principles and fundamental truths. This may not be a static activity. Applying fundamental truths to new challenges requires constant reassessment, discussion, and even argument until new wisdom is forged. Supreme Court justices, ecclesiastics, and good supervisors do this.

Keep abreast of new developments and their implications. This is a more dynamic source of mentoring. It means that a mentor's task of self-development, learning, and mastery is never finished. This need not be a heavy task if we choose specialties such as the evolving mission of our organization or the technology in our given field.

Mentoring is an evolving field. If, as a mentor, you choose to master active listening, coaching skills, effective confrontation techniques, or new methods of resolving conflict, you are starting a journey of self-development.

MENTORING STYLES

There is a need to match mentoring styles to the personalities involved, and to develop your own knowledge, skills, and abilities in ways that are compatible with your personality.

Do you like to philosophize, discuss, and argue interesting points?

_____

What is your response to this type of mentoring?

_____

_____

Do you like to be active, interested in what works, and get things moving?

_____

What is your response to this type of mentoring?

_____

_____

The above questions are a simplified way to encourage you to think about mentor and mentee styles. What type of mentee would you work with most productively?

_____

_____

_____

List three types of self-development you might consider, to become the type of mentor you would like to be.

1. _____

2. _____

3. _____

CASE STUDY: IKA

Ika is a streetwise young man in his late teens who lives in a tough inner-city neighborhood with his mother and two younger brothers. He dropped out of high school, but after a bout with drugs and rehabilitation he managed to get his high school equivalency diploma. Last fall he started taking two evening courses at a community college. He passed both courses with marginal grades, and signed up for two more this semester.

You are the supervisor of the shipping department and Ika's boss. You have noticed that Ika is learns quickly, works steadily, is careful with the equipment and merchandise and occasionally asks penetrating questions about how things are done. He has made several good suggestions about work methods, which you have implemented. You suspect he has several types of talent.

You live in a pleasant suburban neighborhood, belong to the local American Legion Post, coach a boys' softball team, serve as a vestryman in your church and spend the rest of your free time with your family. You have spent 14 years with the company.

Your company plans to automate the materials-handling system in the plant and the shipping department. You have been asked to provide one employee who knows the present system, to serve as a liaison person. That person will work with the consultants who are to study the system and develop changes. Jim, the most experienced person, plans to retire soon. Ika knows the system well enough, but he would have to be coached by you on some details. The three other employees do not appear to be good candidates. Two are fairly new and the other skips work fairly often.

Last week Ika said his studies were getting him down, and wondered aloud whether he had what it takes to graduate college. He said one of his teachers loads them down with homework and does not explain things clearly. He is also discouraged about ever being able to get his family out of "that neighborhood."

(Turn page and respond to this case)

CONSIDER IKA'S CASE

What risks might be involved in mentoring Ika? _____
_____
_____

If you decide to get involved with Ika, what might you plan to do? _____
_____
_____
_____

Considering all the commitments you have, the nature of your work, and the demands of the new project, would you be willing to mentor Ika on a serious basis? _____
_____
_____

If you decided to spend more time helping Ika, what other aspects of your life and work might you consider changing? _____
_____
_____
_____

What if Ika were black and you were white? _____
_____
_____
_____

What if Ika were white and you were black? _____
_____
_____
_____

C H A P T E R

3

Understanding Mentees' Needs

ADAPTING TO CHANGE

Any mentee has some general needs which he shares with others of similar background and situation. He also has his own personal and unique agenda and his own values, perceived limitations, and aspirations. Complicating this highly personal equation is guidance from his mentor and other opinions, desires and events that intrude upon the mentee's daily life.

In mentoring, the mentee is called upon to consider other changes offered by her or his mentor, whether they are generated by a challenging opportunity or a revealing personal insight. For our mentees, change is the name of the game, whether it is self-imposed, a new option, or intrusive.

Managing this change takes place in a constantly shifting personal and organizational environment. There is bound to be a sense of loss from giving up familiar and comfortable beliefs, behaviors, and sometimes even relationships. There is fear of the unknown and of possible failure, even when those feelings are willfully suppressed. Ironically, there is even anxiety when success is achieved—we fear we may not measure up to the expectations placed on us by ourselves and others.

Often a part of the mentor's role is simply to be there for her mentee, to listen, to comfort, to be a friend.

> Recognizing the needs of a person adapting to change, and responding appropriately, is the mentor's challenge.

READING MENTEE SIGNALS

READING MENTEE SIGNALS

The problem messages from our mentee usually contain a *fact* and a *feeling*. "Jack, I've got a financial problem that just won't let go of me" is a factual statement of a person's perception. But it doesn't clearly emphasize the feeling. List three factual statements a mentee might make to signal that he or she was experiencing a problem.

1. _____

2. _____

3. _____

Some problem messages focus on a feeling which is complicating the person's problem solving. "My financial condition is driving me crazy" signals the stress the speaker is suffering. List three "feeling" statements a mentee might make.

1. _____

2. _____

3. _____

Feelings may also be expressed nonverbally—by facial expressions, tone of voice, gestures, or posture. List three nonverbal ways a mentee might signal a feeling.

1. _____

2. _____

3. _____

These feelings are important. They should not be discounted. Statements such as "Don't worry about it," "It can't be that bad," or the cheerful "Everything will turn out all right" are responses which demonstrate that we are not taking our mentee's problem or our mentee seriously.

POSITIVE SELF-IMAGE

We all have a need for confidence and a positive self-image. How we respond to our problems almost always reflects our feelings about ourself at that time or our general perception of self. Research indicates that two-thirds of our population suffers from generalized low self-esteem. They also tend to have negative feelings about specific aspects of themselves or about attributes they possess.

This focus on one's deficiencies makes it difficult for a person to generate the energy, to be motivated, or to make positive changes. A primary role of a mentor is to provide genuine confidence-building insights and experiences.

A less appreciated aspect of damaging one's self-image is the way the mentee talks to or about himself. Virtually everyone carries on an inner dialogue with herself or himself. This self-conversation is frequently negative, focusing on one's failures or shortcomings. Many of us have, in fact, been taught that we should depreciate our achievements rather than revel in them. This pulls down our spirits and our sense of achievement, focusing our thoughts on our failures. Is it any surprise that so few of us make much use of our inherent talents?

It is one thing to suffer a defeat and feel discouraged, but quite another to beat on one's self for it. A mentor can:

- Listen nonevaluatively to the discouragement, thereby giving the mentee a chance to vent her or his negative feelings

- Provide ideas for remedy when asked

- Offer help if the mentee needs it, once the mentee has decided on a problem-solving course of action

BUILDING SELF-CONFIDENCE

Allowing and encouraging a person to talk through his negative feelings enables him to put those feelings behind him. List three specific responses you might make that would keep the ball in your mentee's court without putting him down.

1. _____
2. _____
3. _____

Considering your resources such as position, experience, and contacts, identify three things you might offer your mentee to expand her horizons and/or build her personal confidence.

1. _____
2. _____
3. _____

Suggest three ideas that could help your mentee build a more positive self-image.

1. _____
2. _____
3. _____

How can you and your mentee increase the number and quality of your mutual life-enhancing experiences?

1. _____
2. _____
3. _____

MANAGING CHANGE

When a person is undergoing significant change, she usually needs five things to adapt successfully:

1. A vision of how she and things around her will be when she has changed successfully

2. Time to absorb the new vision

3. Time to adjust behaviors

4. Coping mechanisms to manage the stress of change

5. Time to ponder the meaning of the change, and to internalize and own the change

Context shifting is the key to this process. If a person can clearly imagine what he and his world would be like if he successfully accomplished the desired change, he will begin to do things which move him toward his goals. This mental adjustment needs to be imagined in positive terms, instead of the dread scenarios we often create in our minds. Helping our mentee shift her mental context from today's problems to tomorrow's success can be very productive.

We should not expect instant change. In fact, quick change can be so stressful that pain overwhelms us or encourages backsliding.

Mentees also need a rich variety of healthy coping mechanisms to deal with the stress of change. Mentors help mentees expand their range of positive coping mechanisms and avoid counterproductive ones, such as taking a drink of alcohol when the going gets rough.

EXAMPLE: A laid off steelworker who continues to think of himself as such, may block other options, get discouraged, and turn to drink or drugs. A mentor who helps the mentee envision and become comfortable with alternate futures (such as learning computer skills), may lead to some serious alternatives. This can be a touchy area and some mentors do it badly. Professional help may be more effective.

MEETING MENTEE NEEDS

Think of one valuable change you would like to make in your life. Imagine what you and your environment would be like if you accomplished that change. Focus on positives. Describe this condition:

_____
_____
_____

List three ways you bolster your own self-image:

1. _____
2. _____
3. _____

Identify three ways you use time as a factor in adapting to necessary or desired change (such as developing new skills or knowledge):

1. _____
2. _____
3. _____

List three effective coping methods you use to deal with stress in your life:

1. _____
2. _____
3. _____

Which of these techniques would you be willing to share with your mentee?

_____

Cross out any unhealthy or negative coping mechanisms listed above. You would not want to pass these on to your mentee.

DEALING WITH GRAY AREAS

Helping someone to grow as a person is not always straightforward or simple. A mentee is living her own life, has a variety of demands from a variety of sources, and is changing daily in a multitude of ways. Each day we each grow older, meet new people, encounter new problems and challenges, and perhaps suffer from some defects. No matter how little we seem to change, remaining the same is not possible.

Some mentee adaptations may be noticeable or even dramatic. Others may be gradual and almost imperceptible. Some may be cloaked.

If the mentoring relationship is long-term, the mentor may need to:

- Pick up on subtle concerns the other person begins to articulate

- Notice small or gradual changes which seem significant

- Read verbal and nonverbal signals coming from our mentees

These concerns, changes, and signals can become response points. All of this can certainly be overdone, but such signals can be clues and cues that help is needed. They may even help to bring the problem to the surface of the mentee's awareness or to define an emerging difficulty.

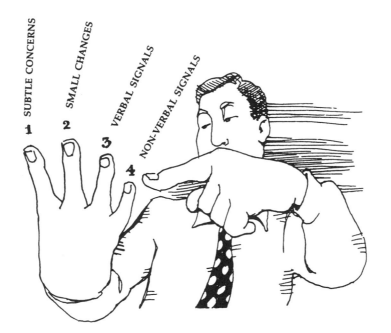

SETTING MUTUAL PARAMETERS

Dealing effectively with small problems to keep them from becoming large ones is a primary way mentors can assist their mentees.

Identify three verbal or nonverbal clues that a mentee might give, perhaps unconsciously, which suggest that he or she is having job or career problems:

1. _____
2. _____
3. _____

Identify three repetitive patterns which might indicate that an individual is experiencing difficulty in his or her long-term personal life:

1. _____
2. _____
3. _____

Identify three repetitive complaints from a mentee that might indicate an unresolved personal difficulty, such as frequently being victimized by others:

1. _____
2. _____
3. _____

Listen for the use of absolutes. They may provide excellent clues such as: "I *never* seem to get along with my bosses," or "He gets to me *every time* we have a conversation." Stated absolutes feel right to the holder but may or may not be accurate. However, recognizing them and discussing them can be a good starting point for identifying and addressing a problem.

CASE STUDY: PAM

Pam is a very bright and sparkling person you met in the company cafeteria. She works for Harold Greening in Accounts Payable.

You have served as an informal mentor to Pam on three or four occasions in the last few weeks, when she wanted to talk about a problem she was having with her finances. You listened, were nondirective in your responses, and gave her information when she asked for it. She said you were very helpful. She also solved her financial problem in a clever way that had never occurred to you.

You have learned that Pam graduated from high school and has also received a certificate in secretarial sciences from a local business school. She seems well trained but not well educated. Her perspective on the world is quite limited, as is her experience. Yet she seems fascinated with the variety and challenges inherent in your job. Her grasp of the difference between your work and lifestyle and hers has led her to talk about changing her life to one more challenging and diverse.

You have heard it said that she is a hard worker and quick to catch on. You believe she is capable of great things, but she seems unaware of her natural intelligence and abilities. This comes out in her conversation—she discounts compliments about her intelligence and ability. She says she is dumb, but everything she does belies that assertion.

You believe that if her self-image and self-confidence were to rise, her talents would become obvious.

(Turn page and respond to this case)

WHAT DO YOU THINK?

CONSIDER PAM'S CASE

If you decide to continue informally mentoring Pam, what special aspects of mentoring would you emphasize?

_____

_____

_____

Would your mentoring be affected if you were a male? How?

_____

_____

_____

How would you attempt to make Pam more aware of her special abilities and talents?

_____

_____

_____

Could focusing on positive self-talk be helpful to Pam? If so, how would you convey the concept and its importance to Pam?

_____

_____

_____

The changes Pam is considering would be substantial, extremely varied and would take a long time to complete. How could you help?

_____

_____

_____

_____

C H A P T E R

4

Positive Behaviors

SEVEN TYPES OF MENTOR ASSISTANCE

Research in several private firms and government agencies reveals seven types of mentor assistance that are particularly helpful in encouraging mentee growth. These are:

1. Helping a person shift her or his mental context

2. Listening when the mentee has a problem

3. Identifying mentee feelings and verifying them (feedback)

4. Effectively confronting negative intentions or behaviors

5. Providing appropriate information when needed

6. Delegating authority or giving permission

7. Encouraging exploration of options

In various ways, these seven items are critical components of life's growth process for all of us. Their strength lies not in any notion that they meet all of the needs of a mentee—they don't. But they meet *key* needs, and when offered at important junctures in a person's life they can help the person resolve a problem or decision and move on.

GROWTH INFLUENCES

Answer only the questions below that you feel comfortable answering.

Is it time for a change? Commonly in life our personal growth begins to strain the bonds of our situation, as when a teen hungers to become an adult.

Identify three situations where a prospective or actual mentee might be ready to move on to a new stage of development.

1. _____
2. _____
3. _____

Think back to an important decision you have had to make in your own life where you were torn between alternatives. List three things you needed from those close to you.

1. _____
2. _____
3. _____

Think back in your life to a point where you made, or were about to make, a serious mistake or error in judgment. Identify three things that someone else did or could have done to keep that situation from turning out badly.

1. _____
2. _____
3. _____

Consider which of these situations could have been beneficially influenced by an effective mentor. What could such a person have done to help you?

_____
_____
_____
_____
_____

SHIFTING CONTEXT

Imagination is a critical component of one's development. The new employee needs to be able to imagine himself as a successful worker in his chosen field, an accepted member of the workgroup, a productive provider for his or her family, or self, or whatever. Constructive imagination appears to be an important component of success in any field or endeavor. By contrast, a gloomy outlook toward one's future often precedes failure.

As mentors, if we help our mentees to create a satisfying new context for their life or work—a personal vision of healthy change—our mentees, on their own, will do most of the things needed to bring this vision to reality.

This art of personal transformation is something we all tend to do subconsciously as long as we continue to mature. But some people get stuck. They rely on outmoded visions and habits. As the world moves ahead, they wallow in increasing obsolescence and possibly despair.

Helping ourselves or others create a personal concept of what excellence in our life would look like, sound like, feel like, and even taste like, can move us toward positive goal achievement. Once we own such an image in our mind, we tend almost automatically to do the things necessary to bring this vision to reality. Successful people tend to use this type of mental creation to guide their path to where they want to be.

Mentors characteristically help their mentees envision worthy goals and move toward fulfillment of such. The notion of context shifting is a developmental art that mentors can share with their mentees.

ENVISIONING OUTCOMES

ENVISIONING OUTCOMES

Before the plan comes the vision.

Carl Ditton had been working as an engineer for 15 years, designing micro-computer circuits for an electronics firm. He was also bored "out of his mind." He was rated as a success and made what he considered good money, but he wanted out.

One day when he was meditating he envisioned himself selling large beauti-ful homes to various people. He was excited by the imagery. He drew up a list of conditions that would be necessary for him to succeed at a real estate sales venture. This was not a plan—he would rely on his creative subconscious to lay out a plan he could follow intuitively. He had the prerequisites. He was articulate, organized and persistent, and he worked well with people.

Later Carl used his list of conditions to imagine himself as a successful real estate salesman selling large, beautiful homes to a host of people, and cashing an abundance of large agent checks. He imagined his family enjoying their spacious home, which he owned outright.

He soon found himself, almost without realizing it, signing up for a course basic to getting his real estate license. Ten years later he was a multi-millionaire, enjoying his work enormously. Carl believed that the secret to his success had been to envision himself in his new role or context so vividly that he could see, hear and feel himself as a successful real estate agent. He could even smell the flowers in the garden of the home he was imagining himself selling.

Envision one personal goal you would like to achieve, which you could personally achieve. Picture yourself being there. Focus on the *what*, not the *how*. Describe what it will be like when you achieve it:

_____

_____

_____

_____

LISTENING

How many times have you served as a sounding board for a friend, relative, or associate when they needed someone to listen to their problems? How often have you wished you had someone to talk to about things that were bothering you? How many times have you experienced the therapeutic release or relief of being able to get something off your chest just by talking it out?

Providing a listening ear, without taking on the other person's problem, giving advice, or joining them in the "ain't it awful" game, can serve as a powerful aid to a mentee. Many mentors believe that respectful listening is the premier mentoring art.

Respectful listening is the ability to become absorbed in what the other person is saying about her problem, treating her words as confidential communication, not injecting our own views, opinions, or suggestions. When respectful listening occurs, the other person has an opportunity to gain insight into her problem by articulating it, to sort things out, perhaps to develop some alternative solution, and almost always to gain emotional release and relief from the quandary which besets her.

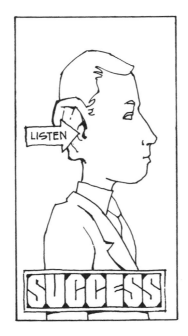

48

ACTIVE LISTENING

Active listening involves engagement with what the other person is saying. It means allowing your mentee to talk without interruptions (unless you must terminate the discussion for some very important reason); accepting what he is saying as genuine, at least to him; and not injecting our own views, opinions, or solutions. Listening to another person for that person's sake is not a discussion. You listen during a discussion, but here we are acting as a helping agent so the other person can unload her or his troubles.

Below are three statements that might be made by your mentee. What is the mentee's message?

1. "When I first joined this organization, I really thought I was going to get somewhere. Well, it's been two years now and I'm still doing the same old thing." Write your perception of his or her message:

_____

_____

_____

2. "This is the type of work I can really sink my teeth into. I get so wrapped up in it I can forget when to go home. Sometimes I lie awake nights thinking about it." What message is the mentee sending?

_____

_____

_____

3. "When I made that presentation on Tuesday, I thought you'd support my position. Instead you only sat there. You didn't open your mouth once. What's a mentor for anyway?" What message is your mentee sending?

_____

_____

_____

Identify the *feelings* your mentee is expressing in each statement:

1. _____

2. _____

3. _____

LISTENING FOR FEELINGS

A primary mentoring function is to help our mentees solve problems they encounter, through listening, counseling, coaching, providing information, exploring options, and *perhaps* through direct intervention—though this should be very rare if we are helping them to stand on their own. These problems most often come to us through statements mentees make during private meetings with their mentors or in counseling sessions. Such messages often provide the context in which mentoring occurs.

In problem messages the feeling is usually more important than the fact, since the feeling mirrors the human concern and is paramount in motivation.

The facts in a message are the objective reality; how a person feels about them usually identifies whether or not a problem exists, the dimensions of the problem, and often its importance.

For instance, "What time is it?" asked in a matter-of-fact voice may reflect a need for information. The same question phrased as "Heavens, what time is it?" and asked with urgency is quite a different message—it indicates a potential problem. The objective facts may be the same in both cases. But the expressed urgency in the second situation may imply a problem that requires action.

Unfortunately, the emphasis we place on facts in our society often diminishes our capacity to recognize other people's feelings, and perhaps even our own. Feelings are important—they motivate our actions—and our inability to detect them may mean we are missing the most important part of the messages people send.

LISTENING FOR MOTIVATION

Researchers on motivation tell us that there are four basic emotions: fear, anger, grief, and joy. These range in intensity from a little to a lot. For example, fear may range from a vague uneasiness to panic; anger may be felt as a small sense of annoyance or uncontrolled rage. Our responses to these emotions may also vary. We may have suppressed a sense of fear or grief within us so deeply that we do not respond until the emotion virtually overwhelms us.

Some emotions are combined with thoughts. The results are such feelings as disappointment, embarrassment, and satisfaction.

The capacity to detect the emotions and feelings of others and to respond appropriately is a critical mentoring art. Since feelings motivate people to do or not do things, ignoring them can limit our effectiveness as a mentor and helping agent. Below are several statements a mentee might make. Identify the feelings and the motivations expressed.

Mentee Statement	Feeling Expressed	Motivation	Likely Action
It seems like a good idea . . . but I just don't know.	_____	_____	_____
I read in the papers this morning that our organization has some serious problems.	_____	_____	_____
I just can't stand that guy—he's a real pain in the butt.			
Nobody promised me a rose garden, but this is ridiculous.	_____	_____	_____
I don't think I'll make it in this program. I'm so far behind.	_____	_____	_____

PRODUCTIVE CONFRONTATION

Sometimes a mentor finds it important to confront the attitude, behavior, or plans of his mentee. To criticize, threaten, or pressure the mentee to adopt another course may lower the mentee's self-esteem. Also, it may be ineffective—the mentee may retreat with her plans or actions. It may also generate resistance, or hurt the relationship.

Communications specialists have found that an "I" message confrontation—an authentic message directly from the mentor—is the most effective way to bring about helpful change in the mentee.

An "I" message generally contains three parts:

1. A neutral description of what you perceive the mentee intends

2. A statement of the possible negative effects on the mentee or other people

3. The feelings or emotions you are having about the mentee's plan

An "I" message works because it *does not* tell the mentee how to behave. The mentee makes the decision.

Once the mentor has confronted the mentee it is appropriate to listen as the mentee works through her problem.

Example:

Your mentee has stated, with determination, her intention to tell off a supervisor in another department, "I'm really going to let him have it."

"I" Messages:

"I'm concerned that you are going to blast Joe, and that such an encounter could badly damage your relationship with his department."

"I don't care, he's got it coming."

"Now I'm concerned that you want to go ahead without regard to the consequences."

52

"I" MESSAGES

Write an appropriate "I" message for each of the three situations described below.

1. Your mentee makes a derogatory remark about a work-group member's ethnic, cultural, or racial origins.

_____

_____

_____

2. Your mentee says mentoring does not seem to be helping him, and he wants to drop the relationship.

_____

_____

_____

3. Your mentee is working full-time and has family obligations as well. She says she wants to sign up for a number of college courses in the fall. You are concerned that the overload could lead to failure and, consequently, discouragement.

_____

_____

_____

Look at your "I" messages again. Do they contain:

- A clear but neutral statement of the problem as you see it?

- A statement of the negative consequences you perceive from the mentee's action?

- A statement of your feelings or concerns about the mentee's behavior or intention?

CASE STUDY: RAY

You are Imelda Rodriques, a highly successful account executive who has, over the last five years, consistently generated the highest earnings for your division. Three months ago you were asked to participate in a formal mentoring program for newly hired recent college graduates. Three months ago you were assigned to mentor Ray Golightly during his first six months on the job.

Ray strikes you as hell-bent on getting to the top as soon as possible. You find nothing wrong with his ambition—it resembles your own. But you question some of his methods.

Ray seems to devote most of his time and energy to making connections rather than demonstrating his abilities through performance.

Ray refers to work assignments given to him by his supervisor as "dummy jobs." He turns in "hastily performed, somewhat sloppy work," to quote his supervisor.

Your company was downsized three years ago, and in the process several layers of management were eliminated. The organization is now lean and mean, with everyone carrying a heavy load. When you explained this to Ray, he saw an opportunity: "Fewer people to get in my way," he responded. He continued to behave as before.

Ray played up to you at first, but Ray interpreted your efforts to help him in ways that meshed with the organization's needs and goals as "getting on his case."

It would be easy not to recommend Ray for retention—and to warn him of your intention—to see if that will induce him to change his ways. But as his appointed mentor, you feel you should make a greater effort to salvage him. You are not quite sure how to go about it, though.

(Turn the page to record your response)

YOUR THOUGHTS

CONSIDER RAY'S CASE

Could Ray's perceptions of corporate life be based on 1980s movies about corporate climbing? Considering the company's downsizing, could Ray's notions be out of date? Give your views:

_____

_____

_____

_____

_____

What mental model does Ray probably have of corporate life? List three or more components of his probable model:

_____

_____

_____

_____

_____

From the concepts and tools discussed in this chapter, develop a plan for mentoring Ray. Outline your plan:

_____

_____

_____

_____

_____

Is internal competition or internal cooperation likely to offer the greatest rewards in our increasingly professional, highly technical society? Explain your view:

_____

_____

_____

_____

CHAPTER

5

Behaviors To Avoid

NEGATIVE BEHAVIORS

Mentors want good things to happen to their mentees. They want them to be effective, productive, achieving, successful, and happy. However, in their eagerness to help their mentees, they may revert to behaviors that prove to be less than helpful. Three such behaviors are:

- Criticizing
- Giving advice
- Rescuing people from their own folly

Dr. Eric Berne, was a psychiatrist and the father of transactional analysis—a method of analyzing human communication to determine its psychological content and intent. He pointed out that these three behaviors are all components of negative psychological games, which involve put-downs of another person, yourself, or everyone in general.

Such games are basically unhealthy. Someone, or everyone, comes out of the game feeling badly—angry, depressed or fearful. Often such games begin with an absolute statement such as "John, you are *always* late, you're *never* on time." These grandiose exaggerations trigger rejection of the message, resistance, and argument. So John's actual behavior—the fact that he's late today—does not get examined or dealt with. These psychological games tend to become endlessly repetitive. The nag continues to nag, the person being nagged resists, and little change in behavior occurs.

Most of us have been taught, at least by example, to criticize, give advice, and rescue people inappropriately. Research on mentoring skills indicate that these behaviors should be offered sparingly, if at all.

"You can't make me do it your way!"

CONSTRUCTIVE ALTERNATIVES

Do you like, enjoy or seek criticism? Even when you ask for feedback on your behavior, do you secretly hope for some favorable information?

List five things another person can do to help you change for the better. Consider personal examples such as losing weight, stopping smoking, etc. Think about how another person could really help you.

1. _____
2. _____
3. _____
4. _____
5. _____

What causes you to feel best when you are making progress toward a significant personal goal? List five things that help your progress.

1. _____
2. _____
3. _____
4. _____
5. _____

When you try something and get in trouble for it, how do you want people close to you to behave? List five behaviors you would like.

1. _____
2. _____
3. _____
4. _____
5. _____

The ideas you have listed are ideas your mentees will probably respond favorably to, when such come from you.

THE PROBLEM WITH CRITICISM

Have you noticed how most people do not take kindly to criticism, even when it is offered as "constructive criticism?"

Criticism is evaluative and judgmental, no matter how we sugarcoat it. When we offer "constructive" criticism, we want our message to be helpful to the other person. But, our intentions are undercut by the way that criticism damages self-esteem, generates defensive blocking, and drains the energy needed for constructive action. Also, if the person accepts the criticism, he acknowledges that he has been bad or wrong—something he is unlikely to do if he is doing wrong intentionally, and something he should not do if he has not been doing wrong at all.

The two most powerful human motivators are survival and security. These motivators are threatened by criticism and evaluation. For some people criticizing, complaining, and nagging are old, self-defeating habits, which tend to prolong the problem. Ever notice how little change results from nagging?

Avoiding criticism does not mean accepting negative behaviors, performance failures, or self-defeating repetitive actions. When a mentee's behavior is not up to snuff, we need to think through an effective intervention.

The key to success is to take new, objective, and creative approaches to encouraging beneficial change, rather than to repeat ourselves endlessly and negatively as critics tend to do. When a person's performance is not up to standard they may need information rather than criticism.

HEALTHY ALTERNATIVES

What are the "thinking" alternatives to automatic criticism? Mentors often give their best when they help their mentees break out of repetitive negative patterns of behavior. When a person makes the same mistake repeatedly, the solution is not to give her the same answer over and over again. The most positive route to change may be to look at the transactions and identify the repetitive elements so these can be changed—even if the change is painful.

For example, if one's mentee has a repetitive performance failure on the job, instead of encouraging her to do better, complaining, or warning her of the consequences, a new analysis of the problem might be helpful.

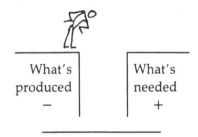

A performance failure can be viewed as the gap between what is needed and what is being produced. This gap needs to be described and measured. A mutual plan needs to be developed for closing the gap so that the problem disappears. Mentor and mentee need to cooperate in problem solving.

What's produced −   What's needed +

Improvement/Change

The performance gap is described in neutral, non-evaluative terms. Closing the gap is viewed as a feat to be accomplished.

Think of three personal or mentee problems you have encountered. Describe them first in evaluative terms, then in neutral, "gap" terms.*

Evaluative Terms	**"Gap" Terms**
1. _____	_____
_____	_____
2. _____	_____
_____	_____
3. _____	_____
_____	_____

* "gap" terms are specific and measureable, often suggesting a way to solve the problem.

THE PROBLEM WITH ADVICE

Many mentors believe that a large part of their job is giving advice to their mentees.

There is a downside to giving advice. When we give advice, we assume we have superior knowledge, insight, or wisdom related to the problem. This may be true when we are engaged in professional discourse.

But when we are dealing with a mentee's personal problem, whether job related or not, our mentee is likely to know more about the problem than we ever will. After all, he or she has been living it. When we attempt to give advice or offer suggestions about personal problems, we often encounter frustrating resistance and a lot of "yes, buts." This should not be too surprising. It is presumptuous and even a little arrogant to assume we know more about another person's problems (even job-related personal problems) than that person does.

Often we can serve our mentees best by:

1. Listening carefully as they describe their problem

2. Feeding back the emotions we hear them expressing, to confirm that we not only heard them but understood the deeper, emotional nature of their difficulty

3. Providing ideas or information, when they ask, which they can use to help weave their own solution

Most independent-minded mentees do not really want advice, though they will value your experience, ideas, knowledge of how things work and special insights into problems. To keep them independent, offer but do not push. They must learn to make their own decisions, if they have not already.

Effective mentors stick with helping. They share, they model, they teach; they do not take over someone else's problems unless there is a crisis which requires immediate action. Mentee growth depends on the mentee solving most of his or her own problems.

INFORMATION VERSUS ADVICE

Dr. Steven B. Karpman proposed the Drama Triangle, a way of analyzing psychological games, which illustrates why people often resist taking advice.

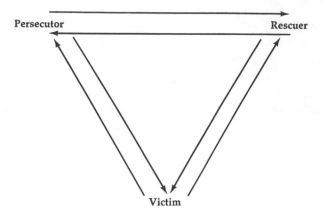

When a person feels victimized by a problem, he may send a plea of "help" to a person he perceives as able to rescue him (i.e., as a person more capable than himself). The victim's feelings of inadequacy are real, but his lack of ability usually is not.

The would-be rescuer accepts the inadequacy of the victim and offers advice. In doing so, she contributes the "why don't you" component to the "why don't you—yes, but" psychological game.

Most often the victim rejects the advice with "yes, but," followed by a reason for not taking the advice. This is hardly surprising, since he knows all of the facets of *his* problem and probably has already considered and rejected all of the easy answers.

The rescuer has only the information that the victim gives in response to each suggestion. She keeps making suggestions, each of which is rejected for some seemingly new reason.

Finally, the rescuer grows impatient with the rejections and turns persecutor. She says something to the effect of, "Buzz off—you don't really want to solve this problem."

At that point each party is confined in his or her own judgment. The victim feels even more like a victim. He not only still has the original problem, he also has the would-be rescuer exasperated with him. The would-be rescuer has confirmed his belief that the victim was and still is inadequate. The victim is also convinced that his problems are too big to be solved by anyone. And the relationship has been damaged.

THE PROBLEM WITH RESCUING

The world is full of genuine victims, people who through no fault of their own come upon hard times. Often these people need help, as when a hurricane strikes, or there is an auto accident, or when an employer goes out of business.

Another type of victim also needs help, but perhaps a different type of help. Some individuals, because of feelings of inadequacy, prior victimization, or maladaptation to crises in their lives, set up repetitive patterns of failure. Most of us do this in some areas of our lives. If we have not experienced actual failure, we may fail to achieve all that we are capable of.

When dysfunctional patterns of behavior occur in the mentee's personal or work life, a mentor can help by pointing out the repetitive nature of the transactions. The mentor can use counseling skills to help the mentee break the pattern.

Rescuing the mentee, or attempting to take over the problem, is not likely to be helpful in the long run. Temporary help in a crisis may be appropriate, but when there is a recurring pattern of such rescuing, the mentor becomes part of the mentee's problem.

MISDIRECTED HELP

Mentoring should be a pleasant, satisfying experience. When we get annoyed, suspicious, or anxious, our negative feelings are first-class clues that something is amiss. They signal a need for problem identification, definition, and resolution. In each of the following mental statements, identify the feelings to help define the nature and magnitude of the problem. Then identify what you would consider a typical intervention or response. Then indicate a constructive response based on material in this manual.

1. "I think the intern program is a waste of time. It isn't doing me any good and I want to drop out of it."

Feeling: _____

Typical Intervention: _____

_____

Effective Response: _____

_____

2. "Once again I thought I had a chance to really make it, and once again I've failed."

Feeling: _____

Typical Intervention: _____

_____

Effective Response: _____

_____

3. "It seems like I can never get ahead. My finances are a mess, I've got bill collectors after me all the time, and I just don't know what to do. I may even face bankruptcy."

Feeling: _____

Typical Intervention: _____

_____

Effective Response: _____

_____

CASE STUDY: EDDY

Eddy Chang recently graduated from a first-class engineering school. He joined your department less than a year ago. He is amiable and well-liked by his co-workers. His engineering qualifications are impressive, and there have been hints that his talents could be considerable once he gets his feet on the ground.

You are Jim Backus, his technical supervisor. You are the lead designer and have been with the organization 12 years. You have spent considerable time teaching Eddy as much as you could, but you have a hard time understanding his speech. And he sometimes seems to have trouble understanding yours.

Eddy's family migrated here from Southeast Asia several years ago. Relatives sponsored his family in the United States, and Eddy was able to complete most of his high school and college here with good marks.

By working very hard at it, Eddy can present his ideas adequately in writing, but his verbal presentations are disastrous. His presentation of the results of a piece of work to an in-house weekly symposium was a bomb. His overhead slides were overloaded with equations, he mumbled as he read his notes, he failed to look at his audience, and he presented his verbal information in a sketchy, abbreviated fashion.

Some of the participants dozed, some read other materials, and a few in the back talked among themselves. During the question-and-answer time, not one question was raised. You were embarrassed both for Eddy and for your colleagues and their behavior.

Later your manager asked you to mentor Eddy as well as supervise him. Since you had been teaching him the work as fast and as well as you could, you thought you had been mentoring. When you pointed this out, your boss said, "No, this goes beyond doing your job. Try to be a friend to him, help him to succeed. Do what you can to turn him into a winner."

(Record your response on the next page)

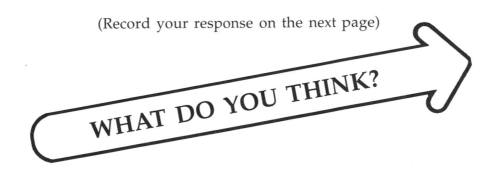

WHAT DO YOU THINK?

CONSIDER EDDY'S CASE

List what you see as Eddy's obstacles to success:

_____

_____

_____

_____

_____

_____

What cross-cultural problems may be lurking?

_____

_____

_____

_____

_____

_____

List some ideas as to how you might help Eddy (especially ones that might be "going above and beyond").

_____

_____

_____

_____

_____

_____

_____

_____

_____

_____

C H A P T E R

6

Mentor-Mentee Gains

GAINS

1. MUTUAL RESPECT
2. EMPOWERMENT
3. FRIENDSHIP
4. CAREER SUCCESS
5. PRODUCTIVITY

PARTNERSHIP

Mentoring is often perceived as a one-way street, with the mentor giving and the mentee receiving. In the past, this top-down, parent-to-child relationship was often based on the assumption that the mentee was not in a position to do much in return except be a dutiful and appreciative protégé.

It was difficult to engage in adult-to-adult communication, even though the mentee often was of age. In organizations the mentor was usually a senior person and the mentee was his or her junior. This reinforced the giver-receiver aspect of the relationship. The senior/junior relationship seemed so natural that few people questioned the assumptions on which it was based.

In the past this often worked, giving career success to the mentee and a type of parental satisfaction to the mentor. But it tended to produce clones and prepare people to succeed in a world which is now passing. In these days of self-empowerment and rapid organizational and professional change, the senior-junior model needs revision.

Today, mentoring may be viewed as a partnership, with both parties freely contributing to the discussion as equals working together, based upon mutual respect. A mentor may still have greater experience, insight, and wisdom, but the relationship can be one of showing (even material showing) rather than only top-down giving and receiving. After all, the mentor *helps* but the mentee *does*—or the relationship is a failure.

MAKING THE MOST OF THE RELATIONSHIP

Mentoring is not a bookkeeping exercise. There is no need to balance accounts or to give back in kind. Yet, a two-way flow of kindness, respect, or giving can return much to the mentor. In the spaces below, explore ways that giving can flow freely in the relationship.

From the mentor's perspective: *things you would like to get from the relationship—candor is critical here.*	From the mentee's perspective: *things a mentee could contribute to the relationship.*

ANTICIPATED GAINS

As a cultural value, we extoll selfless generosity. We give for love—of our mate, our children, our parents, our neighbors. This giving is usually honest and sincere. But since we also have needs, we hope that others will apply the golden rule and that some joy will come our way. If it does not, we may be disappointed and possibly resentful.

Acknowledging that each of us also has needs and being open and honest about them can help us to make our expectations explicit. Failing to state our expectations of another person is all too common and unfair. Mentees and mentors need to be explicit about what they hope to gain from the relationship. This helps both parties determine if the match is likely to be a good one.

ASSESSING PERSONAL EXPECTATIONS

As a mentor, what do you hope to get in return for your investment in time and effort?

1. Types of satisfactions? _____
   _____
   _____
   _____

2. Types of recognition and from whom? _____
   _____
   _____
   _____

3. Types of rewards? _____
   _____
   _____
   _____

4. Other benefits or returns? _____
   _____
   _____
   _____

5. Would you be willing to share these hopes or expectations with your mentee? _____ If not, why not? _____
   _____
   _____
   _____

DETERMINING MENTEE EXPECTATIONS

A few mentoring relationships end badly: in anger, in quarreling, in disappointment. As with nasty divorces, these traumatic partings often result from unmet expectations on one or on both sides. Some expectations may be buried deeply in a person's culture or upbringing, such as perceptions of what a man is supposed to do or what a woman is supposed to be like. Expectations may be subconscious and never surface until a quarrel erupts.

For example, since the mid-1980s many firms have been downsizing their operations as well as laying off large numbers of midlevel managers and professional workers. Several stories appeared in print about people complaining that their mentors failed to take care of them. "When the going got rough he worried more about his own career than he did about mine," complained one young professional.

It is unlikely that the mentors and mentees had ever discussed whose career came first. Yet the persons being mentored had that expectation and levied it on their mentors without making the assumption explicit. If the persons being mentored had been called protégés and had been told they would be helped in their career advancement by their mentors, the assumptions levied on their mentors might make sense.

Efforts should be made to address mentee expectations before the relationship begins, during mentee training, in exploratory talks between mentor and mentee, and through mentee small-group discussion. Mentor expectations should be similarly developed or expressed—at least during mentor training—and shared with their mentee openly.

CHECKING MENTEE EXPECTATIONS

CHECKING MENTEE EXPECTATIONS

Three methods of ascertaining mentee expectations are:

1. Ask the mentee to write a brief essay of one or two pages describing what he or she expects to gain from the relationship—short-term and long-term.

2. Ask the mentee to identify briefly his or her perception of the roles and responsibilities of each party in the relationship.

3. Ask the mentee to list any special needs or features of the relationship that should be considered in developing the relationship.

This exercise is especially valuable if the mentor is developing similar data, rather than simply reacting to the mentee's work. Unwillingness to make one's assumptions explicit may be a set-up for future conflict and misunderstandings.

It is important that the mentor not overreact to the mentee's expectations. Most often they are an honest statement of expectations gleaned from the mentee's background and his or her notions about mentoring. If the mentee's expectations are more than the mentor is willing to accept, they should be negotiated.

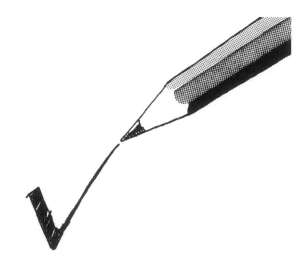

DEVELOPING A MENTOR-MENTEE AGREEMENT

When formal mentoring arrangements are established, usually sanctioned by the employer, school, or other agency, a mentor-mentee agreement may be helpful.

When both parties to a mentoring relationship have made their expectations clear, reconciliation of views may be necessary. At least they should define how they will work together and what they hope to achieve through this association.

Their agreement need not be formal or even written down. Any effort to set up a potential "I gotcha" is probably unhealthy. Mentoring is, at its foundation, a friendly, helping, informal relationship; any effort to extract promises is probably based on fear, mistrust, or hostility.

The goal of their agreement is to set objectives for their mutual effort. It is a tentative agreement, subject to change as required. It is mutual, in that both parties should benefit in satisfaction and happiness.

From the days of the medieval craft guilds to today's apprenticeships and training programs, there have been agreements between mentors and their mentees. Some are written; most are not. Whether written or verbal, what each person is willing and able to invest in the relationship initially should be clearly worked out and agreed upon, as well as what outcomes they expect. The greatest value of developing such an agreement and making it explicit comes from the freewheeling discussion between mentee and mentor. An accepting demeanor in these discussions is essential.

TESTING A MENTOR-MENTEE AGREEMENT

In formal mentoring, every agreement has key points which indicate how well it is working. Depending on the nature of the agreement, these key points need to be checked periodically. Mentor and mentee should discuss points that should be amended, dropped, or improved. One system that works well seems to be a thirty-day checkup, a ninety-day review, and a six-month examination, which can be repeated every six months indefinitely. Of course, any problem should be dealt with when it arises.

What are three key points that a mentoring agreement might contain?

1. _____
2. _____
3. _____

How might these key points be adjusted in a thirty-day checkup?

1. _____
2. _____
3. _____

In a ninety-day review?

1. _____
2. _____
3. _____

In a six-month examination?

1. _____
2. _____
3. _____

CASE STUDY: MARY JANE

Mary Jane is seventy-two and hasn't missed a day of work in over thirty years. She is cheerful and helpful to everyone, performs well, and says she expects to be around until she's a hundred and ten. Mary Jane thrives on hard work. She participates in several civic and charitable activities and takes one college course a semester—usually in a professional subject, but occasionally she signs up for a "fun course." Pictures of her grandchildren and great-grandchildren adorn her office credenza.

Recently Meg Rose announced she will retire in seven months. The next day Mary Jane asked you to help her prepare for Meg's job. She is amply qualified and has the seniority—though seniority here is more a custom than a rule. She noted that you have successfully mentored several women, and though you are not in Meg's chain-of-command you know a lot about her work that would be helpful.

You are a corporate vice president, the most successful woman in the corporation. You have broken many historical taboos about women's careers. You could provide unique insight into Meg's job and its relationship to the work of other departments. However, Kurt Smith, Meg's supervisor, doesn't take kindly to other people's involvement in his area.

Mary Jane has told Kurt she is interested in Meg's job. He was surprised and commented on her age. She shot back that his remark could be the basis of an age-discrimination suit, but that she wanted to win the job by her proven ability and her record. She reportedly left Smith gasping for breath. The Federal Age Discrimination in Employment Act and a state law allow Mary Jane to continue working indefinitely, as long as her performance is up to standard.

Mary Jane also told Meg she wanted to be her successor. She said, "Succeeding in your job would be the crowning feather in my career cap." Meg likes Mary Jane and is probably mentoring her. However, Mary Jane has told you clearly that she wants to "earn that job."

(Turn page to record your response.)

RECORD YOUR THOUGHTS

CONSIDER MARY JANE'S THOUGHTS

Considering the politics, should you agree to mentor Mary Jane? _____

_____

_____

_____

_____

What would you be willing to offer Mary Jane as your mentee? List as
many items as possible. _____

_____

_____

_____

_____

Would actively listening to Mary Jane in detail be appropriate here? _____

_____

_____

_____

_____

Identify any items that should be part of a mentoring agreement you might
make with Mary Jane. _____

_____

_____

_____

_____

What personal rewards might you derive from mentoring Mary Jane? _____

_____

_____

_____

_____

CHAPTER

7

Special Situations

IDENTIFYING SPECIAL ISSUES

Now that you are familiar with mentoring in many of its ramifications, list ten areas in your organization where formal or informal mentoring could be helpful.

1. _____   6. _____

2. _____   7. _____

3. _____   8. _____

4. _____   9. _____

5. _____   10. _____

Consider how competition, changes in your organization's mission, or other external factors are affecting the future of your organization. Identify ten trends that could have an impact on you and other employees.

1. _____   6. _____

2. _____   7. _____

3. _____   8. _____

4. _____   9. _____

5. _____   10. _____

Identify three ways in which mentoring might be used to influence the organization's future and that of the people within it.

1. _____
_____
_____

2. _____
_____
_____

3. _____
_____
_____

NEW AREAS OF MENTORING

In recent decades, mentoring has been used for an increasing variety of people, situations, and purposes.

In academic environments, mentoring has been used to stimulate and motivate gifted students, to acclimate minority students to college life and its challenges, and to provide help by older students to younger students in specific subjects. Government agencies have provided technical mentors to recently graduated new hires in professional fields, assigned mentors to personnel just entering the executive ranks, and trained senior personnel as mentors to facilitate an agency's adjustment to increased workforce diversity. Private firms have begun to use mentoring as an instrument for organizational development (not just as a career development tool), as a method for adapting the organization to competitive challenges, and for succession planning.

Informal mentoring is also taking on a wider variety of forms and is serving a growing host of mentee needs. In-country mentors are helping globally mobile businesspeople adapt to unfamiliar cultures, mores, and legal codes. And the list of applications is growing.

The three special mentoring situations given in this chapter—cross-gender, cross-cultural, and supervisor or manager mentoring—are examples of the diverse applications of mentoring. They represent the three primary challenges in mentoring when it is used to adapt our workforce to demographic changes already underway, to prepare us to operate in a competitive global environment, and to manage organizational and technological change effectively.

SPECIAL ISSUES

CROSS-GENDER MENTORING

Until recent decades, cross-gender mentoring in organizations has been rare. Several studies of mentoring reveal a number of problems related to cross-gender mentoring based on gossip, envy, suspicion, speculation, false assumptions, sexual stereotypes, and charges of sexual harrassment. Unfortunately, such attitudes and behaviors have lessened the effectiveness of cross-gender mentoring in some environments. Yet, each sex has much to offer and teach the other. Cross-gender mentoring can leaven the workplace, enrich the lives of mentees, and provide valuable insights and experiences to each sex.

A gender-balanced and fairly treated workforce is likely to remain a challenge rather than a reality for some time. Effective cross-gender mentoring is one of the tools we can use to achieve this balance and fairness.

CROSS-GENDER (continued)

List five advantages to the organization or to society from cross-gender mentoring:

1. _____

2. _____

3. _____

4. _____

5. _____

If you were to mentor someone of the opposite gender, what unique skills might you offer him or her?

1. _____

2. _____

3. _____

4. _____

5. _____

If you were to mentor someone of the opposite gender, what unique skills might you learn from him or her?

1. _____

2. _____

3. _____

4. _____

5. _____

CROSS-CULTURAL MENTORING

Look around you. Signs of cultural diversity are virtually everywhere. This diversity represents some of the most subtle and special relationships imaginable. Even in relatively homogeneous societies, differences in economic class, religious background, regional allegiance, and even family traditions can generate cultural differences which can complicate the task of mentoring.

Cultural differences and our personal response to them are a large part of what makes each of us unique. Our cultural uniqueness may also enable each of us to appreciate special facets of a problem, approach its solution from different angles, and contribute to a more comprehensive, elegant, and lasting solution. As we move from a society of things to one of human values, mentoring offers a powerful tool for benefiting from cultural diversity. By carefully listening, by respecting our differences, and by practicing the art of inclusion, we can build a stronger, more rewarding organization and society.

CROSS-CULTURAL (continued)

When we go to a restaurant, attend church, listen to music, watch a movie, go to work, speak to another person, play games, dance, or receive medical treatment, we can hardly avoid enjoying advantages which are based on diverse contributions of people from all over the world. We can trace the origin of a plate of spaghetti to China, modern medicine to the ancient Arabs, the roots of Christianity to the Hebrews of old, modern dance rhythms to Africa, or the Tex Mex meal we have just enjoyed to the ancient Toltecs of Mexico. Our lives have gained richness and variety from people all over the world, whether we are aware of it or not. The contributions are almost endlessly varied.

Identify five ways in which different cultures are currently contributing to our society.

1. _____

_____

_____

2. _____

_____

_____

3. _____

_____

_____

4. _____

_____

_____

5. _____

_____

_____

MENTORING BY A SUPERVISOR OR MANAGER

Some of the most powerful, effective, and long-lasting mentoring can be done by the person who has authority over the mentee—and this can include parents. The power or authority to reward and punish people creates both opportunities and obstacles to effective mentoring.

The possession of power or authority over a mentee can work against a helping, caring, nurturing relationship. It is difficult for a mentee to become her own person when she is subject to pressures from others.

Yet power and authority need not be used negatively. Used wisely, to challenge, to offer opportunities, and to encourage, power and authority can provide powerful assistance to a mentee. The mentor can model a proper use of personal power—of voice, of literary skills, of persuasion. The power of expertise and the power of judgment can provide valuable learning opportunities for a mentee.

Mentoring by a supervisor or manager must be done carefully, artfully and fairly. If you mentor subordinates, mentor all of them. In one respect, bringing out the best in each employee may well define the art of supervision. Mentoring can contribute strongly to the development of that art.

THE ISSUE OF HIERARCHY

Hierarchy is not simply a matter of placing people on an organizational ladder. We have hierarchies of knowledge, of experience, of seniority, and yes, of position and power. Hierarchies of influence, personal complexities, and abstraction also exist.

List three ways you, or someone you know of, are able to influence others through avenues that are not related to layers of organizational structure:

1. _____

2. _____

3. _____

THE ISSUE OF HIERARCHY (continued)

Rank has an obvious relationship to hierarchy. But rank can blind us to more subtle relationships in mentoring and can cause us to be misled. Identify one or more people you respect and admire who rank highly in your estimation in the following areas:

Integrity _____

_____

Sensitivity to others _____

_____

Consideration of others _____

_____

Moral or ethical leadership _____

_____

Loyalty _____

_____

Any other area _____

_____

Write down three ways you can use your power or influence to help a mentee—whether you thought of that person as a mentee or not—to broaden his or her horizons, experience reasonable challenges, or understand a special facet of his or her work or activity:

1. _____

_____

2. _____

_____

3. _____

_____

SUMMARY

You can make mentoring formal or informal. It's up to you! It can be a long- or short-term investment, a single action or an agreed upon plan. The success of your relationship depends upon the commitment you and the mentee are willing to make to meet the challenges and capitalize on the opportunities.

The rewards are great and we hope this book has helped you identify the practical aspects of assessing, developing, and maintaining positive mentoring behavior.

Happy Mentoring!

NOTES

NOTES

NOTES

NOTES

NOW AVAILABLE FROM CRISP PUBLICATIONS

Books • Videos • CD Roms • Computer-Based Training Products

If you enjoyed this book, we have great news for you. There are over 200 books available in the *50-Minute*™ Series. To request a free full-line catalog, contact your local distributor or Crisp Publications, Inc., 1200 Hamilton Court, Menlo Park, CA 94025. Our toll-free number is 800-442-7477.

Subject Areas Include:

Management

Human Resources

Communication Skills

Personal Development

Marketing/Sales

Organizational Development

Customer Service/Quality

Computer Skills

Small Business and Entrepreneurship

Adult Literacy and Learning

Life Planning and Retirement

CRISP WORLDWIDE DISTRIBUTION

English language books are distributed worldwide. Major international distributors include:

ASIA/PACIFIC

Australia/New Zealand: In Learning, PO Box 1051, Springwood QLD, Brisbane, Australia 4127   Tel: 61-7-3-841-2286, Facsimile: 61-7-3-841-1580
ATTN: Messrs. Gordon

Singapore: 85, Genting Lane, Guan Hua Warehouse Bldng #05-01, Singapore 349569   Tel: 65-749-3389, Facsimile: 65-749-1129
ATTN: Evelyn Lee

Japan: Phoenix Associates Co., LTD., Mizuho Bldng. 3-F, 2-12-2, Kami Osaki, Shinagawa-Ku, Tokyo 141   Tel: 81-33-443-7231, Facsimile: 81-33-443-7640
ATTN: Mr. Peter Owans

CANADA

Reid Publishing, Ltd., Box 69559-109 Thomas Street, Oakville, Ontario Canada L6J 7R4.   Tel: (905) 842-4428, Facsimile: (905) 842-9327
ATTN: Mr. Stanley Reid

Trade Book Stores: *Raincoast Books,* 8680 Cambie Street, Vancouver, B.C., V6P 6M9   Tel: (604) 323-7100, Facsimile: (604) 323-2600
ATTN: Order Desk

EUROPEAN UNION

England: *Flex Training,* Ltd. 9-15 Hitchin Street, Baldock, Hertfordshire, SG7 6A, England   Tel: 44-1-46-289-6000, Facsimile: 44-1-46-289-2417
ATTN: Mr. David Willetts

INDIA

Multi-Media HRD, Pvt., Ltd., National House, Tulloch Road, Appolo Bunder, Bombay, India 400-039   Tel: 91-22-204-2281, Facsimile: 91-22-283-6478
ATTN: Messrs. Aggarwal

SOUTH AMERICA

Mexico: *Grupo Editorial Iberoamerica,* Nebraska 199, Col. Napoles, 03810 Mexico, D.F.   Tel: 525-523-0994, Facsimile: 525-543-1173
ATTN: Señor Nicholas Grepe

SOUTH AFRICA

Alternative Books, Unit A3 Micro Industrial Park, Hammer Avenue, Stridom Park, Randburg, 2194 South Africa   Tel: 27-11-792-7730, Facsimile: 27-11-792-7787
ATTN: Mr. Vernon de Haas